Retain and Gain

Career Management for Small Business

Lisa Taylor, Challenge Factory

ceric

CANADIAN EDUCATION AND
RESEARCH INSTITUTE FOR COUNSELLING

INSTITUT CANADIEN D'ÉDUCATION
ET DE RECHERCHE EN ORIENTATION

CANADIAN EDUCATION AND RESEARCH INSTITUTE FOR COUNSELLING
INSTITUT CANADIEN D'ÉDUCATION ET DE RECHERCHE EN ORIENTATION

Retain and Gain: Career Management for Small Business

Published by:
Canadian Education and Research Institute for Counselling (CERIC)
2 St Clair Avenue East, Suite 300
Toronto, Ontario
M4T 2T5
Canada

Website: www.ceric.ca
Email: admin@ceric.ca

ISBN
Paperback: 978-1-988066-17-2
EBook: 978-1-988066-18-9

Acknowledgements:
This Playbook was published by CERIC (the Canadian Education and Research Institute for Counselling). CERIC is a charitable organization that advances education and research in career counselling and career development, to increase the economic and social well-being of Canadians.

After consultations with its Board of Directors and the Marketing, Communications and Web Services Committee, CERIC turned to career expert, author and small-business Owner Lisa Taylor to research and write this guide for you, Owners and Managers in small businesses (those with fewer than 500 employees). As the Founder and President of Challenge Factory and the Centre for Career Innovation, Lisa is widely recognized for her "future of work" insights while also managing a growing business. She is passionate about the changing nature of careers and the resulting impact on the economy and on people of all ages.

Lisa would like to acknowledge the following leaders, advisers, research subjects and contributors:

Sharon Ferriss, CERIC's Director, Marketing, Web and New Media, is an inspirational project leader and Norman Valdez, CERIC's Senior Manager, Digital Media & Communications, is a talented and creative designer. Thanks are also due to CERIC's visionary leaders Riz Ibrahim and Bruce Lawson, President of The Counselling Foundation of Canada. The project also benefitted from the research support provided by Daniel Mester, Cayla Charles and Ian Munro.

Lisa and Sharon would also like to acknowledge the support of the project's Knowledge Champions:

Jennifer Hagan from the Canadian Chamber of Commerce, Richard Buteau and André Raymond from Laval University, Dr. Marie Bountrogianni and Fred Anger from The G. Raymond Chang School of Continuing Education, Ryerson University, Ian Young from The CFO Centre, and Anthony Kellner at TD Bank Group.

This project was guided by a fantastic advisory committee, with thanks to the following members: Fred Anger and Dr. Marie Bountrogianni, The G. Raymond Chang School of Continuing Education, Ryerson University; Jenny Basov, Toronto Regional Board of Trade; Beth Dea, Futurepreneur; Don Edmonds, Edmonds Rose; Sue Folinsbee, Tri En Communications; Jennifer Hagan, Canadian Chamber of Commerce; Anne Lamont, Maritha Peens, André Raymond, Laval University; and Mark Venning, ChangeRangers.

Lisa would also like to acknowledge the organizations that participated in our research interviews. These organizations all have fewer than 500 employees, are located across Canada (coast to coast to coast), represent Anglophone and Francophone ownership and are in the private, public and non-profit sectors:

Ian Young, CEO, The CFO Centre; Taffik Choudhury, Managing Director, Traxion Strategic Partners; Derek Bullen, Owner, S.I.Systems; Vanessa Melman Yakobson, CEO and Partner, Blo Blow Dry Bar; Joan Garson, Baskin Financial; Mary Aitken, President and Founder, Verity, George, Sweetgrass Spa and The Ivy; Don Coady, Owner & Creative Director, DC Design House; Nancy Rowland, VP Corporate Services and Operations and COO, Ontario Science Centre; Shirley Zerfas, Owner, One Imaging Inc.; Rona Birenbaum, President, Caring for Clients; Sheldon Kreiger, Owner and Operating Partner, Boston Pizza; Chantelle Hansen, Director of Human Resources, JMP Engineering; Scot Rutherford, President and CEO, Scot Builders; Jillian Hardie, Executive Director, Challenge Disability Resource Group; Vanessa Légère, Consultant in Development of Competencies and Processes, Victrix; Jenny Basov, Senior Manager, Human Resources, Toronto Regional Board of Trade; Roxanne Larouche, Director of Human Resources, Yukon Hospital Corporation; Jeff Quipp, CEO, Search Engine People; Laura Ambrozic, President, Mimic Print; Eric Walker, Managing Partner, CW Partners LLP; Geneviève Babin, Vice President, Groupe Pro Sante; Guylaine Gélinas, General Manager, Provincial House of the Ursulines of Quebec; Steven Thériault, General Manager, Matelas Dauphin, and additional interviewees who wished not to be named. ∎

CONTENTS

Section 1: Introduction

Note to Business Owners

Congratulations! By picking up this Playbook you are among the select group of Business Owners who know that there is a direct link between healthy employee careers and strong business results.

Business ownership is a journey for those seeking adventure, fulfillment, surprise, growth, satisfaction and reward. And, while it may sometimes feel like you are alone in your exploration, it is far from a solitary path. In Canada, 99.7% of all business with employees are small- or medium-sized enterprises (SMEs), with the vast majority of organizations falling into the category of the "micro business," (10 or fewer employees).[1] In fact, in 2015, SMEs employed 90.3% of the private sector workforce (10.5 million Canadians).[2]

Success depends on great products or services, strong client relationships and a solid understanding of your market. Staying on top of day-to-day operations while planning for longer term strategic moves is critical. There is no shortage of work to be done, nor is there a limit to who needs your time and attention.

But, there is a shortage of time and, in many cases, capital to do all of the things that you want to do. That's what makes the SME Owner's journey unique. It requires focus and creativity in how you use the resources you have available to you.

In 2015, the Business Development Bank of Canada completed a study to determine what SMEs needed to successfully grow. They presented their "Winning Strategies" after thoroughly profiling Canada's small- and medium-sized enterprises, including analysis and recommendations for talent-related challenges that inhibit growth.

In examining the BDC report, we noted the following finding:

"Clearly, the size, industry, age and location of a business are all factors that influence its ability to grow. However, these factors will have no impact if the business's leaders do not wish to expand in the first place."[4]

This Playbook is your opportunity to reconsider how you think about

DID YOU KNOW?
On average, employee-related costs account for an estimated 70% of overall operating costs. The relationship you have with your workforce is both your most significant risk and your greatest competitive opportunity.[3]

6

DID YOU KNOW?

We asked Business Owners which people-related issues keep them up at night:

- 83% worried about engaging and retaining employees
- 66.7% indicated finding the right talent and recruitment was a challenge
- 61.1% were concerned about developing new leadership candidates and Managers
- 50% wondered how to provide career development opportunities for employees throughout their careers with limited opportunities for promotion
- 50% worried about compensating and rewarding employees (although only 38% of respondents indicated they were worried about managing tight salary budgets in a competitive market)

When these results were analyzed by age of company, we found that finances were most concerning for companies within their first 7 years of business. Recruitment concerns increase for companies with 4-7 years in business. By the time a company has been in business 7 or more years, employee engagement, retention and leadership development concerns dominate.

invested your staff are, personally, in the success of the business. We assert that there is nothing more personal than each employee's individual career. More than one-off rewards or team-building exercises, focusing on your team's careers ensures that your business will succeed because they've succeeded.

Indeed, career management affects more than just employee satisfaction and loyalty. It drives better customer service, faster identification of ways to improve business operations and increased opportunity for growth – for employees as well as for your business. ∎

career management as a strategic lever for stronger company performance. We'll provide key statistics, tools and tips throughout the Playbook. To get started on this journey, consider the following from the Temkin Group [5]:

Highly engaged employees are:

- 2.5 times more likely to stay at work late if something needs to be done after the normal workday ends
- More than twice as likely to help someone at work even if they don't ask for help
- More than 3 times as likely to do something good for the company that is not expected of them
- More than 5 times as likely to recommend that a friend or relative apply for a job at their company

Employee engagement is a way to express how

TAKE ACTION:

Throughout this Playbook you will see the "TAKE ACTION" heading with some suggested ways to take the information in this Playbook and put it to immediate use. Don't feel like you must incorporate all suggestions or topics covered immediately. The aim of this Playbook is for it to be an ongoing resource you can use over time.

Note to Managers

Welcome to the Career Management Playbook designed for you - a smart, engaged and curious Manager.

TAKE ACTION:

The templates, resources and tools are provided to guide you to action. If something doesn't quite fit, feel free to change it. We hope that the ideas are a starting point that inspire you to grow and build your people through great career experiences. As a first step, you might want to share this guide with the Owner of your company (or have them get their own copy) and work through key topics together.

In developing this Playbook, we spoke with Managers in SMEs across Canada. From British Columbia to Yukon to Newfoundland we heard about limited time and a need to play many roles. Some commented that if they had the responsibilities they currently held and worked in a large corporation they would have a much larger title with greater market understanding of their skills and experience. Others expressed sincere concern for the careers and, indeed, the lives of their employees and struggled regularly to do right by them while still managing cash flow and workload demands of the business.

As we created this Playbook we noted some significant disconnects between what Managers and employees think about current career patterns. Specifically, we noted that:

- 60% of HR leaders believe that their companies provide employees with a clear career path – and only 36% of employees agree that this is true. [6]

- 82% of Millennials say that they are loyal to their employers, but only 1% of HR managers would use the word "loyal" to describe their Millennial staff. [7]

- 68% of employees say their Managers aren't actively engaged in their career development. [8]

Even Managers who believe they are well connected with their staff and are helping with career development may find that their employees do not recognize that they are being supported. The disconnect between Manager intention and employee experience can often lead Managers to disengage from career management activities. After all, if efforts to assist employees go largely unused or unappreciated, there are other priorities and ways to focus precious time. The result can be a spiral of disengagement among staff.

Consider yourself a traveller and this Playbook is your travel guide. Keep an open mind about what you might find and learn as you explore new ways to engage with your staff. You may find that this journey is not at all what you expected and that there are specific activities, off the beaten path of common management wisdom, that create exceptional experiences for you, your staff and your company. ∎

Why Use a Travel Guide Format

As a SME Owner or Manager, you know 1 thing for sure: there is never enough time to do what needs to be done.

We heard this loud and clear while completing the research for this Playbook. Business Owners told us over and over again that they believe they have the knowledge and skills to be better career advisors and Managers for staff. They have the know-how, but lack the time and are unsure how career management applies in a flat structure. Many felt that while they provide employees with "jobs," there were limited career development opportunities for staff, and discussions would only lead staff to look at other companies for a next career step.

It got us thinking, where else do we encounter new, unknown experiences with an overwhelming number of activities that could and should be done, and limited time? How can we provide a fresh approach to improving the careers of those who own and work within SMEs? We learned that we need to provide a business-focused Playbook that gives Owners and Managers what they actually need:

The gift of time and proven action steps that fit into your everyday work schedule.

You will find we have structured this Playbook in an innovative and creative way. We learned in our interviews and research that you value access to career resources that you can immediately use. There was a clear interest in a brief Playbook that helped in everyday interactions and activities, with links to recommended resources and more detailed support for those interested in taking a deeper look into a particular topic.

For these reasons, we structured this Playbook like a travel guide.

When we travel we are limited by the amount of time we can spend in any single location. We need to make the hours count and stretch our financial resources as far as possible. It is all about the experience.

Similarly, time and resources are critical constraints for Business Owners and Managers. You know that recruitment, employee engagement, employee retention and productivity depends on positive employee experiences including opportunities to learn, grow, be recognized, be challenged and be rewarded. But how do you make good on the promise of a great employee experience while juggling tight budgets, limited staff and not enough time to do all of the things that "should" be done.

Why Use a Travel Guide Format
continued

The right "Career Management Itinerary" will deliver experiences that meet the needs and aspirations of both your staff and your business.

We will show you that career management is a high-value, high-return, low-risk business lever that will carry your business across long distances. And, really, who doesn't love taking a "just for you" custom-designed trip? ∎

TRAVEL TIP: LEARNING THE LANGUAGE

Travel often involves learning new terms. In our research, we learned that SME Business Owners and Managers believe "career development" and "training" are synonymous, while the term "career management" was generally understood to be broader, encompassing many different activities and lasting for a person's full working life. Small organizations also felt that "talent management" and career management were the same thing, while medium-sized organizations tended to view talent management as a strategic corporate activity, which might not include providing career-focused tools and assistance to staff. Throughout this Playbook we will use career management to describe our topics and activities, although some of the quoted sources may use other terms. For our purposes, we will consider career management and career development to have the same meaning. For those interested in formal definitions, career management is "a lifelong, self-monitored process of career planning that focuses on choosing and setting personal goals and formulating strategies for achieving them." [9]

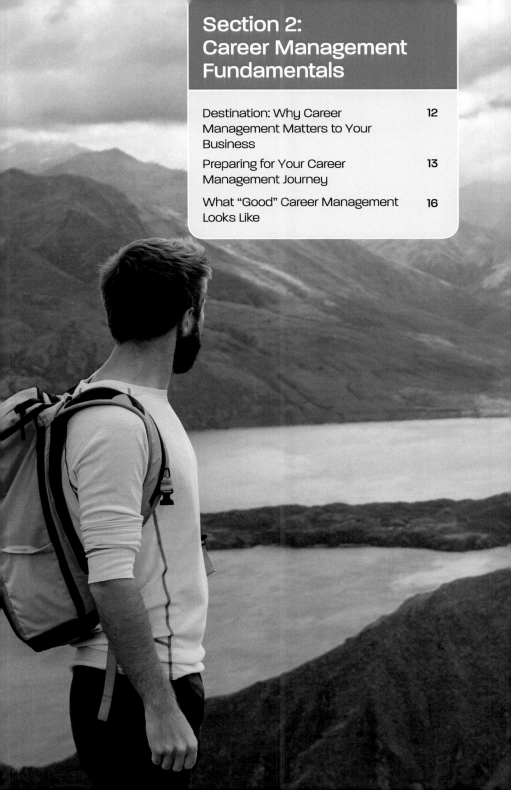

Section 2: Career Management Fundamentals

Destination: Why Career Management Matters to Your Business

Employees want to know you are invested in their careers. You need a strong team and employer brand. Ongoing career management is the answer.

This section provides background information to help you become familiar with the language, opportunities and options that career management offers your business. In a real travel guide, this section would be your overview to the city, province, state or country that you were going to visit. If you would like to jump right into planning your company's customized career management plan or itinerary, you can find templates, activities and tips starting on page 20. ■

DID YOU KNOW?

We asked SME Owners and Managers what image best represents how careers work. Here are the top 10 images that came to the Owners' minds:

- "Mountain range where peaks lead to the next valley and a new peak"
- "Kids maze where there are many entrances and 1 of them leads to the path that reaches the centre"
- "Staircase"
- "Paths with many branches to choose from along the way"
- "Group of mountain climbers who support each other and provide equipment to help at various stages of the climb"
- "Safari, because you don't know what wild animals lurk in the weeds and rivers you have to cross because you haven't reached them yet"
- "10 years ago, it was stairs, but now people can have so many careers it's hard to say but a trip or a journey most describes it"
- "A pyramid"
- "A ladder"
- "Trains - sometimes you get derailed"

VOICE OF AN EMPLOYER

"When employees see that we invest in them, that there is the possibility for career development, they stay. And even if they leave, they come back." [10]

Preparing for Your Career Management Journey

Career management activities will enhance business results, with minimal advance preparation.

TRAVEL TIP:
Some trips are planned all on our own. Others are more complicated or require insight we don't have the time to gather. In these cases, we turn to travel agents and tour companies to help us plan a great experience. In the field of career management there are advisors and experts able to help you with planning and execution. Look for professionals who use the term "career" (distinct from "HR") to describe their area of expertise.

Before preparing for a trip, most people have a few specific questions:

- What can we afford?
- When is the best time to travel?
- What type of experience do we want to have?

In preparation, you plan, budget, scour online review sites and ask friends about cities, hotels and tours. You then make choices that best fit your criteria.

Similarly, your current and future employees go through the same process when deciding to apply, join or stay with your company. They consider the salary and benefits offered and whether now is the right time in their career to have the role that you are offering. But, more than any other factor, they evaluate what it is like to work with you.

Does the day-in, day-out experience of being on your staff energize and build their career or does it drag them down? What is your workplace culture?

In this Playbook, we provide tips and activities that enhance career opportunities, that build your culture and that establish a strong employer brand.

Anyone who has been through a recruitment cycle knows just how time consuming it is to recruit and hire new employees and how important it is to make good hiring choices.

And hiring is just the beginning. SMEs struggle to maintain employee engagement and to retain top performers. We learned in our interviews that many SMEs experience high turnover among top performers due to a perceived limit on career advancement

Preparing for Your Career Management Journey continued

opportunities.

But we know that there are many opportunities for people to grow their careers, in meaningful ways, even in a flat or small workforce structure.[11]

Employees need to have a broader understanding of their own career, while Owners and Managers need to motivate, challenge and support employees as they grow. How these needs are identified, met and measured in large part defines the culture of your company.

Like any country, territory or city, your company has its own culture and it is often informal and unstated. Even a stated mission, values & vision statement does not prevent your employees from talking with family, friends or online about what it is like to work at your organization. Indeed, the "way business is done around here" does not always align with how Owners or Managers would describe desired corporate culture. Your brand as an employer is

TRAVEL TIP:
As you explore the rest of this Playbook, consider the growth path that your company is on. You likely know what your goals are in terms of revenue and profit. If you have equipment, you also likely know what investments you will need to make to increase production, reduce repair costs and minimize risk. But what are your employee-related goals and investment plans?

We couldn't create a Playbook for SMEs without referring to the number 1 issue that keeps Business Owners up at night: cash flow. While employees often wish their employer would pay for additional training or send them to industry events, we know that cash-related pressure is intense, especially in the first few years of being in business. Therefore, the core activities, tips and major recommendations provided in this Playbook are designed to work with free (or low-cost) resources. From time to time we mention additional services that you might want to invest in, but only as an option. Every trip has financial limitations and even budget travellers can have incredible experiences.

Consider these questions as you evaluate the ROI of spending time and/or resources on career management activities:

- What costs are we incurring by ignoring or deferring the career needs of our staff? **HINT:** It costs you in hard dollars as well as lost productivity

- When is the best time to start improving employee engagement? **HINT:** NOW

- What type of employee experience and employer brand do we want? **HINT:** One that engages and motivates staff to do their best work

just as important as the brand(s) you maintain for your products and services. Today it is easy for staff to share what they love and regret about working with you on social media sites like LinkedIn and Glassdoor,

for prospective staff, partners and customers to see.

Engaged employees align their own career success with the success of the brands and organizations they work for. How your employees perceive opportunities within your company is linked to key business results. Turnover is expensive and members of a disengaged workforce will not be the brand or customer advocates you need to differentiate from your competitors.

Cash flow is the critical issue for SMEs. However, in study after study, career management is at the heart of priorities 2, 3, 4 and beyond. From recruitment to onboarding to retention and management, the employee career lifecycle is important to both the employee and the business.

In fact, challenges with finding and retaining qualified and engaged staff contribute directly to your company's ability to better manage its costs. Consider Gallup findings that demonstrate higher workplace engagement leads to 37% lower absenteeism, 41% fewer safety incidents and 41% fewer quality defects.[12] ■

DID YOU KNOW?

- Career satisfaction and work-life balance have been identified as the top 2 reasons employees stay at their current jobs. [13]

- 78% of employees said they would remain longer with their employer if they saw a career path with the current organization. [14]

- 55% of SMEs expressed difficulty hiring and retaining qualified personnel, making it the second greatest challenge to growth only after dealing with growing operating costs. [15]

What "Good" Career Management Looks Like

SME Owners shared with us their concerns about having career conversations with staff.

Some worried that they would not be able to offer good suggestions. Others misinterpreted career management for performance management and resisted having to have hard discussions about shortcomings and consequences. Still others worried that encouraging broader career discussions would only encourage key employees to leave for opportunities in larger companies.

Good career management requires that Managers and employees understand certain fundamentals about their careers. CERIC has developed its **8 Guiding Principles of Career Development** to help clarify and define the scope of career-related work. (Recall that we are using the terms career management and career development synonymously for this Playbook).

These principles can help ensure you have good career-focused conversations, resources (like those listed at the end of this Playbook) and programs in place with your staff.

Career Development:

1. Is a lifelong process of blending and managing paid and unpaid activities: learning (education), work (employment, entrepreneurship), volunteerism and leisure time.

2. Entails determining interests, beliefs, values, skills and competencies – and connecting those with market needs.

3. Involves understanding options, navigating with purpose and making informed choices.

4. Should be self-directed; an individual is responsible for his or her own career, but is not alone – we all influence and are influenced by our environment.

5. Is often supported and shaped by educators, family, peers, Managers and the greater community.

6. Means making the most of talent and potential, however

VOICE OF A BUSINESS OWNER

"10 years ago [careers were like] stairs, but now people can have so many careers it's hard to say but a trip or a journey best describes it."

DID YOU KNOW?

Performance management is not the same as career management. Performance management is "an ongoing process of communication between a supervisor and an employee that occurs throughout the year, in support of accomplishing the strategic objectives of the organization." [16] It focuses on how well employees have accomplished specific job-related activities in support of stated business goals. For example, is the sales person meeting his or her target? Is the project Manager staying on time and on budget? In our research, most companies have a method or system for performance management and we will assume that your employees are performing and meeting company targets. This Playbook will address topics and actions that go beyond performance-related discussions, interventions and follow-on actions.

you define growth and success – not necessarily linear advancement.

7. Can be complex and complicated, so context is key – there may be both internal constraints (financial, cultural, health) or external constraints (labour market, technology).

8. Is dynamic, evolving and requires continuous adaptation and resilience through multiple transitions.

Career management principles, theories and tools are not necessarily included in entrepreneurship or human resource programs and, while there are many HR-focused resources for SMEs, most have a heavy emphasis on compliance.

Career management resources and experts tend to come from the public (policy-focused), academic (research-focused) or non-profit (service delivery-focused) sectors. However, as career paths change in today's innovation and, increasingly freelance-enabled economy, SMEs and larger enterprises are seeking guidance from new, yet very established, sources. Career management provides decades of wisdom and results to help leaders and employees navigate today's changing employment structures.

Career management is not a solitary pursuit. Managers play a key role alongside individual employees. This relationship has been described in Chapter 16 of the text *Career Development Practice in Canada: Perspectives, Principles, and Professionalism,* by Sandra Boyd and Kim Spurgeon as a career partnership, in which:

"Managers, by providing learning opportunities and supporting career goals, help to empower their employees and further their career development. The organization, for its part, has a duty to help develop employees' career-management skills through human resources programs, mentoring, and networking. Lastly, the employees themselves must be accountable for their own development through self-assessment, skills updating, and setting career goals. When these three work together, employees become more engaged and retention improves." [17]

Indeed, good career management has a strong link to high productivity, faster time to market and higher customer satisfaction. It is led by

What "Good" Career Management Looks Like continued

the individual, can take many different forms and is not necessarily focused on promotion or mobility. Instead, it is rooted in the understanding that career development occurs when employees have increasing access to unique experiences. ∎

DID YOU KNOW?: TOP 10 MISCONCEPTIONS ABOUT CAREER MANAGEMENT IN SMEs

Based on our interviews with Canadian SME Owners and Managers, we heard the following misconceptions about career management. They are all false and prevent companies from establishing good career practices. How many are at play in your organization?

1. Small companies can offer jobs. Careers are only possible inside large enterprises.

2. Career management and training are the same thing, as are career development and advancement.

3. Employers are in control of the career paths of their employees.

4. Staff know how to manage their own careers.

5. Managers know how to help staff with their careers.

6. Millennials are more interested in lifestyle and work-life balance than a traditional career.

7. Older employees don't need to worry about their career as they are unlikely to make a significant change after age 50.

8. Career management is costly and doesn't deliver an immediate return on investment to the business.

9. Career management is only for professionals or knowledge workers.

10. There isn't hard data, proven practices and solid research available to help SME Owners and Managers. with tough career related situations.

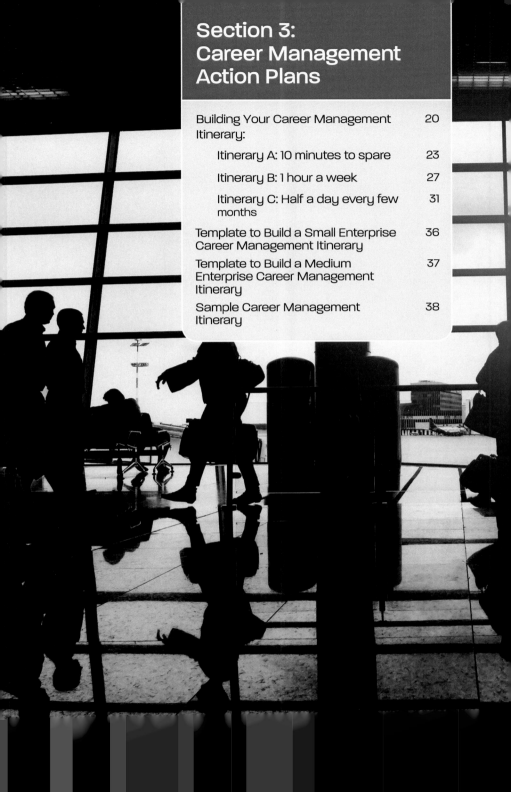

Section 3:
Career Management Action Plans

Building Your Career Management Itinerary

So far, we've focused on making the case for career management within SMEs and providing some guidelines on what good practices and programs might consider.

Using a travel analogy, we've provided background on the career management practices that develop employees and build business success (the "destination"). We've also outlined how career management can make your organization a more attractive place for recruits.

But we all know that the most rewarding part of preparing for a trip occurs once the itinerary is set and the planning is done; when you know what to expect and can focus on how to make an already great schedule a terrific experience.

In our research, we learned that organizational size matters when it comes to how time is spent. We learned that companies with 1-50 employees deal with limited time and resources differently than those with 51-499 employees. We also learned that the perceived career management skills of Managers as well as the priority they place on career-related coaching and support differs by size of company. Therefore, we've provided you with 2 templates to use as you select which activities you want to include in your company's customized Career Management Itinerary, 1 for companies with 50 or fewer employees and 1 for companies with 51-499 employees. ∎

For Companies with 1-50 Employees:

You operate with the most limited time, capital and employee resources. Your business requires you to be both leader and foot soldier and every hire that you make needs to perform. You are more informal than larger companies when it comes to HR policies and procedures and the Owner of the company likely performs most of the employee performance and career management activities.

In our research, we learned that Business Owners and Managers in companies with less than 50 employees are more likely to be able to plan additional activities if they are done on a weekly or monthly basis. When you do find extra time in your day, it is last minute and requires activities that can be completed quickly without having to draw in other people.

For Companies with 51-499 Employees

Your business has a bit more equilibrium than the smaller-size companies. There is more stability and confidence in your future growth capabilities, especially if you have been in business between 5-8+ years. You likely have adapted your original organizational structure so that there are team leads or Managers who assist the Owner(s) with day-to-day employee performance management, even if the senior leadership team is still actively involved on a quarterly, bi-annual or annual basis in performance reviews and workforce/recruitment planning.

Our research identified that approximately 67% of Owners and Managers in mid-sized companies do find an hour of unaccounted for time within a typical week, more than what is reported by Owners and Managers in smaller companies. You also are more likely to have formal career or performance review cycles, either quarterly, twice a year or annually.

TRAVEL TIP:
You will find a template for small companies (1-50 employees) on page 36 and for medium-sized companies (51-499 employees) on page 37. As you read through the suggested career management activities, you can use these templates to build your own "itinerary" or customized action plan.

TIPS TO GET YOU STARTED

1. Just as a travel guide would have different categories of recommendations (hotels, tours, dining, transportation, etc), we, too, have considered that you may want to build your Career Management Itinerary based on various types of activities.

   - For some, focusing in on 1 goal might lead you to complete the activities across a specific activity (like a "Foodie" Tour would emphasis dining options as priority activities).

   - Others, might look to balance what is included in their plan to get broader exposure to career management across a variety of activities – like a "Cultural Highlights" Tour.

   - Finally, others might skim each activity and select only those that tie specifically into a current business issue. In this case, the analogy might be a themed trip where most of the lodging, dining and touring events focus on a specific topic or theme.

2. Like when planning a trip, we have listed far more activities than can reasonably be accomplished within the likely timeframe that you want to set, such as a 6- to 12-month period. Don't feel pressure to choose more than the number of activities you feel is realistic (perhaps with a few extra in case you become particularly engaged or priorities change). Just as you can't see everything in a city or country in 1 day, you can come back and build new itineraries each year to broaden your career management experience and exposure.

3. The activities are structured to start at the top by challenging you to think differently, with each subsequent section becoming progressively more action oriented and tied to business goals. We recommend starting by reading all the activities and putting a star beside or circling the activities you want to come back to. Next, review the activities you have "shortlisted" and consider which are most important and what order you wish to tackle them. Then, fill in the itinerary template provided.

4. In addition to the activities listed that are relevant to all businesses, others are provided which are better suited to companies with 51-499 employees.

Itinerary A:
10 minutes to spare

If you have 10 minutes to spare you might choose 1 of these activities. You can do the same activity each day, or alternate between a few activities.

 Think About

Goal: Identify new, positive actions to take

Think about yourself.
Identify one career defining moment from your past. Write it down and consider sharing it as part of an upcoming team event, call or communication. Why was it meaningful? What did you learn?

Does your story provide context to any business or career situations others might be experiencing? If so, consider sharing your story as part of a broader employee communication.

See the Travel Tip for good employee communication on page 25.

 Share

Goal: Develop a culture of collaborative learning that encourages employee development

Begin to regularly share 1-line success messages with your staff that highlight how an employee has grown or developed new skills. Consider using this format:

Subject: Career Creativity

Body: Last week [employee name] showed career creativity when they helped [customer/peer/me] solve a problem. [Outline the problem and what it meant to the person and to your business]. I look forward to [employee name] sharing what they learned from the experience. Well done.

DID YOU KNOW?

According to the Canadian Research Working Group on Evidence-Based Practice in Career Development (CRWG), "For the most part, employees of small and medium enterprises enjoy their work and like working for a small company. They value communication with their employer and co-workers a great deal. However, they feel limited with regard to possible development and, together with their employer, would like to be able to identify new challenges." [18]

TRAVEL TIP:

We asked Small Business Public Relations Expert Keka DasGupta of www.kekadasgupta.com for her advice should you find that your employees are expressing workplace or career frustration online. Here is her brand-protecting recommendation:

"No matter how wonderful your offering may be, when it comes to online ratings, people know there will always be a select few who will complain. But positive ratings must vastly outnumber negative ones for us to accept an offering as great. It's all about ratio. Consider TripAdvisor. Some of the world's best hotels have both good and bad reviews on the site. When we see many more positive reviews in comparison to negative ones, we are reassured.

Similarly, to neutralize negative employee reviews online, SMEs must proactively communicate positive messages about their company to external audiences.

Here are some ways to do this: 1) encourage employees to become authentic ambassadors of the company by sharing their experiences online; 2) share company principles and values publicly, so external audiences can see what you stand for; 3) build your public profile so people get to know you and like you as a leader."

Itinerary A: 10 minutes to spare continued

Some organizations will send these "success" messages out whenever there is a success to celebrate. Others will set a more predictable schedule, perhaps including these messages as part of a broader monthly or quarterly communication. Whatever frequency you decide to use, let your staff know what they can expect and ensure you spend 10 minutes every few weeks soliciting stories from staff and Managers.

 Discuss

Connect the dots to align business goals to the day-to-day experiences of the team

Call a staff member and have a "check in" with no agenda. Let them know you are calling to see what's new with them and check in on their day. Be clear that you have about 10 minutes and if a longer conversation ensues you will schedule a follow-up time to address items in more detail. Let them spend a few minutes sharing whatever information is top of mind for them.

What you discuss does not have to be "career" related – but know that there are career implications for building this type of casual rapport and relationship with your staff. In regions where staff have long commutes, you may find the last part of their drive into work is a good time for this type of casual "check in" – although every employee is different.

After the discussion, note priorities, topics or questions that come up.

Select a different staff member next time.

Do

Goal: Take action that fosters career opportunities for your team

Search on LinkedIn and Glassdoor to see how your employees are talking about your company and brand. Identify 2-3 people you want to talk to about what you learn to get an outside perspective and support. How can you share the good messages you see?

If there are negative comments, you will need to address them from 2 perspectives. First, you need to determine what course of action is appropriate for the employee. Action might include anything from speaking with the employee to dismissal. However, keep in mind that mild messages of discontent provide an excellent learning opportunity for both the employee (how could they have found a better, more direct outlet to express what they need) and for you (what doesn't your company know or do well that should get more attention).

See the Travel Tip with suggestions for managing your online employer brand on page 24.

Reflect Upon

Goal: Take time to focus on what you and your team need to keep growing

Select a quote from this list of over 1,001 entrepreneurial quotes compiled by Canadian entrepreneur Bruce Firestone: **https://www.amazon.ca/Quotes-Entrepreneurs-Great-Inspire-Motivate/dp/1496011252** and consider how it can apply to you and your team.

Here are some of our favourites to get you started:

"Any intelligent fool can make things bigger, more complex, and more violent. It takes a touch of genius—and a lot of courage—to move in the opposite direction," Albert Einstein.

"Standing is more tiring that walking," Paradox.

"It always seems impossible until it's done," Nelson Mandela.

Measure

Goal: Identify good data that can help you make better business decisions

Most Business Owners felt that training and career management were the same activity. They aren't. Training can be 1

TRAVEL TIP:

When launching new initiatives or programs with employees, you will need to think about who should be eligible for these opportunities and how you will communicate to the team. According to Priya Bates of Inner Strength Communication, good employee communication considers "3C's" – Contact (who, how frequently, what method), Content (what you want to share and when to share it) and Context (being authentic and considering other explicit and implicit messages being received). You can find additional resources on internal or employee communications here: **http://ow.ly/VBCz1oosfLk** or **at https://www.iabc.com/.**

tool an employee uses to manage and navigate their career.

Ensure that, from now on, your staff complete an evaluation of any online, in-person or on-the-job training taken. The focus should be on what was learned, how it has been applied and how it advanced a

business and a career-related goal. MaRS provides a template for evaluation that you may want to modify or use:

 https://www.marsdd. com/mars-library/ training-evaluation-sample-feedback-questionnaire-for-trainees/.

Book time in the next

month to review the results and consider which training approaches lead to faster improvements in your key business metrics (revenue, cost containment, customer satisfaction, cash flow, etc). ▪

VOICE OF A BUSINESS OWNER

"I worry about managing my communications with the employees. When situations occur, there isn't anyone giving me advice and I don't know where to get support. I have to provide solutions."

Itinerary B:
1 hour a week

If you have 1 hour a week, you might choose to do 2 or 3 of these activities or identify a few activities to include in your quarterly review.

Think About

Goal: Identify new, positive actions to take

Think about the importance of listening to staff and reflecting on their concerns. Consider which questions, priorities and issues

issues routinely emerge in discussions with your staff. Which career-related needs seem to be company-wide and which are unique to an individual or small group of employees? List 3 questions you have about the issues and consider asking more questions in a future 10-minute check

---

Recommended additional activities for companies with 51-499 employees

Think about the role your people Managers play. What development or exposure have they had to career-related tools and theories. Everyone assumes their direct Manager can provide good career guidance. However, most career discussions focus more on job fit either for the current role or for roles in the future. Job fit is just 1 element of a career discussion. It would be like relying on a Manager who knows the requirements and capabilities of specific social media tools to create your long-term strategic marketing plans. Before jumping to which tools fit you would have a more strategic discussion.

Similarly, as you start to manage a larger workforce, there are strategic concepts, frameworks and tools that can help you make better investments and develop stronger career Managers within your organization.

For example, how many of these concepts are familiar to you:

- change management
- life stage/life course theory of careers
- positive psychology
- brain science of the workplace

It is ok if these terms aren't familiar. Your core business is (likely) not in the career development field.

When you have needs in other non-core business areas you look externally for free and affordable resources. There are career management resources available to help build your internal competency with coaching, career conversations, career path development and employee engagement.

Consider if this is an area that should be added to the development goals for your people Managers and who else within your company might help be a "Career Champion."

Itinerary B: 1 hour a week continued

in with an employee or Manager.

Share

Goal: Develop a culture of collaborative learning that encourages employee development

Share an article or tool that focuses on soft skills that are critical to your employees' success. You may want to subscribe to *CareerWise*

which brings a weekly summary of career-focused articles from a variety of sources on timely topics to your inbox: http://www.contactpoint.ca/careerwise. You can then use these weekly summaries to identify 1 article or topic that you would like to share with your staff.

Good sources for career-related articles could be the careers section of your daily newspaper, *INC* magazine, *Fast Company* magazine or LinkedIn Groups (search for "career" and your industry to get access to relevant discussions and resources).

Discuss

Goal: Connect the dots to align business goals to the day-to-day experiences of the team

Discuss what you are working on and your top priorities for the next month. Explain how your work aligns with the work that your staff is doing. Solicit questions that listen for common interests, curiosities or issues. Discuss new

opportunities for your staff to learn from each other, share their work differently and/or explore a new topic that they do not fully grasp but is related to your business. Let them know that you'll ask them to share their findings from these group learning sessions at an upcoming meeting.

Do

Goal: Take action that fosters career opportunities for your team

Focus on retention. Keeping good employees is critical to small businesses and how you lead the team has a lot of sway on how long they will stay with you.

Often Owners of small businesses have close relationships with staff. Over time, discipline around communication and respecting work-life boundaries, etc. may slip as Owners know that they can count on staff to understand what needs to be done and go the extra mile. But everyone needs to know that their efforts are recognized and that their future matters.

Consider how much attention you are paying to your company's culture, to open communication and to being flexible. Has your focus or stance on these topics shifted over time? Do you think your employees know why you have made changes that affect how they interact with you and each other?

For additional tips, consider this article on enhancing employee retention:

📄 **https://www.marsdd. com/mars-library/ retaining-top-talent-employee-retention-strategies-for-startups/.**

Create a plan to implement relevant tips

within the next month.

 Reflect Upon

Goal: Take time to focus on what you and your team need to keep growing

Reflect upon career-related videos and podcasts. TED has some terrific material that challenges us to reconsider how we communicate (Mark Bowden's "The Importance of Being Inauthentic") and how we value happiness and positivity in the workplace (Shawn Achor's "The Happy Secret to Better Work").

Both of these TED Talks challenge commonly held assumptions and include practical tips to try.

There is also a seemingly limitless list of podcasts that can provide you with an ability to reflect on your current business needs and opportunities as it relates to your employees, their engagement and their careers. I especially like: "HR for Small Business" podcasts 📄 **https:// itunes.apple.com/ us/podcast/human-resources-for-small/ id533673516?mt=2.**

And the "Best Part of My Job" podcasts which feature different people sharing their career stories:

 http://www. bestpartofmyjob.com/ podcast/.

Measure

Goal: Identify good data that can help you make better business decisions

What career-related metrics or goals do you set for your staff? Do they have to demonstrate that they've learned something over the course of the year? Do you identify new skills or competencies to acquire or demonstrate greater maturity? How do they align with your business goals? What goals would your employees want to also measure and track? List your top business goals and consider how the career plans of each of your staff might make them qualified or interested in helping you with a special project to focus on 1 of the following:

- Cash Flow
- Increase Revenue
- Decrease Costs

- New Product Development
- Commercialization of Research
- New Partnerships
- Increased Market Awareness
- Geographic Expansion

What else would you add to this list?

With limited time, funds and personnel, which activities promise the strongest ROI:

- Peer mentoring with a knowledgeable expert?
- More frequent career conversations?
- Experiences such as attending trade shows or community events?
- Training?
- Time-bound job shadowing?

The purpose of this activity is for you to start considering various career-related actions and activities in terms of your business goals so you can make good trade-off decisions. ■

DID YOU KNOW?

According to Gallup, "Employees who get the opportunity to continually develop are twice as likely to say they will spend their career with their company." [19]

Recommended additional activities for companies with 51-499 employees

Having Managers and executives who can build a business case and demonstrate how employee-related programs can be measured is an important capability as your business grows. In the busy day-to-day world we invest in programs that can demonstrate strong, hard returns. **Consider asking your finance or accounting staff to help you put together an ROI model** that identifies good metrics to use when evaluating people-focused investment decisions. Rely on their expertise to help you define what is actually measurable, how you would measure it and how you can collect the data needed.

If you are interested in having staff take a training course where a basic model will be developed, consider Course 103: Workforce Program ROI and Analytics at: 🔗 **http://www.centreforcareerinnovation.com**.

Itinerary C: Half a day every few months

If you have a half day every few months or as part of your annual business planning activities, you might add the following: (choose 2 or 3 activities a year).

Think About

Goal: Identify new, positive actions to take

Think about how you motivate your staff. It is sometimes assumed that money is the only motivator – but the research indicates otherwise! What type of experience or exposure would be meaningful to each employee? Some may value attending an event with you. Others might want to be challenged to solve a new type of problem. Create or revise a plan to motivate staff without relying on financial rewards. You may want to consider what rewards might enhance:

- Public recognition – in your company, in your industry, in your community. How can you

showcase great work in your marketing or employee communications? Can an employee represent your company at a public event?

- Workplace – some of your employees will really value items that make their work environment special. What visual reward can you provide?

- Interesting work – is there a unique project or new area to explore? Which staff would love to spend an hour or 2 helping with something different than their everyday work?

For more ideas and suggestions, you may want to refer to:
https://www.marsdd. com/mars-library/ motivating-employees/.

Consider that 89% of employees would consider a lateral move

within their company. [20]

There are also online tools and assessments you can have your staff take to identify their motivators. A free test is available here:

http://testyourself. psychtests.com/ testid/3153.

(Author's note: I prefer to use the assessments provided by TTI. There is a per person fee for the assessment, but I've found them to be accurate, practical and easy for Managers and employees to use).

Recommended additional activities for companies with 51-499 employees

Think about network development. Can you identify three employees (a Triad) from different departments who should know each other? Perhaps they work in different parts of your company and could become a cross-functional team. Perhaps some of your staff have well-developed internal and external network connections, while other staff members might have specific skills or life experience to share. There is strong evidence that suggests if these Triads come from different generations, intergenerational knowledge transfer and innovation emerges faster than in most formal 1:1 mentoring programs.

Itinerary C: Half a day every few months continued

 Share

Goal: Develop a culture of collaborative learning that encourages employee development

Establish a regular schedule to have a career conversation with your staff. Most employees value having

DID YOU KNOW?: TRIADS AND INTERGENERATIONAL MENTORING

"Why triads? Research shows that corporate cultures are shaped by the relationships small groups of employees build. Natural, interconnected networks of people come together and disband continually in the context of work and social relationships. In a high-performing triadic relationship, everyone gives and gains with common, often unspoken, values at the core of the work. Each person is clear about the specific expertise they can offer. They are also tuned into the health of the relationship of the other two parties in the triad. Triads provide a stable yet dynamic structure to implement learning, change and growth programs in the context of the actual working environment. In today's inter-generational workforce, they offer a unique opportunity to align onboarding, leadership development and succession management." From Challenge Factory's *Triadic Mentoring Handbook.*

a monthly or quarterly check in. Ensure employees know the frequency and stick to the schedule. Skipping these meetings conveys that their careers and engagement is not a priority for you. When preparing for a career conversation, you might want to ask the employee for topics that are important to them. Keep in mind that job performance issues or concerns should be addressed as they arise and are not the focus for these more strategic career management conversations.

You will find a guide for both you and your staff here: **http://www.**

crwg-gdrc.ca/crwg/index.php/resources/career-conversations.

You may also find this article helpful:

 https://www.fastcompany.com/919177/dont-run-career-conversations.

If you are looking for additional resources, consider this book by Beverley Kaye:

 https://www.amazon.ca/Help-Them-Grow-Watch-Conversations/dp/1609946324. Or course 105: Better Career Conversations for Managers from:

 http://ow.ly/hh2B1o0uNXj

? Discuss

Goal: Connect the dots to align business goals to the day-to-day experiences of the team

Discuss career-related topics when getting together with other Business Owners. We heard from Managers and Business Owners that they are often part of networks or small groups that meet regularly. For some, this is formally structured as part of networking organizations. Others simply try to meet for coffee, lunch or after work with trusted colleagues.

Arrange a meeting with 3 or 4 other Business Owners or Managers who are not competitors. Discuss how you might collectively support the career growth and development of your teams. Consider sharing success and challenge stories, having staff spend a day shadowing each other to get broader business exposure or identifying business priority projects that you can work on together, such as evaluating new systems/tools or developing a common training class. Set out clear expectations, investment $ available (if any), timelines and responsibilities.

If you are unsure how to get started with this small group discussion of peers, consider approaching your local Chamber of Commerce to help make introductions to other business leaders who would be a good match.

Do

Goal: Take action that fosters career opportunities for your team

Review your current organizational structure. Do you have good, relevant job descriptions?

Good job descriptions include a minimum of the following:

- A headline that would make the ideal candidate jump out of their seats with excitement. This gives you a good "gut

Recommended additional activities for companies with 51-499 employees

Implement an employee triad program where 3 staff members can come together to develop a stronger network (internal and external), develop their skills and support each other's career-related activities. To get started, identify (or have people self-identify) to be part of the first groups of 3.

Itinerary C: Half a day every few months continued

check" that people are in the right role. If it doesn't excite, you need to find out why.

- A description of general duties and what the role is accountable for (Budget? Client relationships? Marketing campaign results?) Make sure you can measure these.

- The competencies needed to do the job well. Three examples of competencies are "Foster Teamwork," "Oral Communication" and "Analytical Thinking." Here is a list of 31 competencies that you can select from: ⃗**http://www.workforce.com/2002/09/03/31-core-competencies-explained/**.

- Finally, you want to include how you know the job has been done well. What are some of the results that would happen if the employee did a great job?

Based on the competencies and measures of success, you can start to consider how employees might build their own career pathways, even in small companies.

A career pathway ensures that employees know that their career will move forward within your company. Often, small companies believe that because there are limited positions and relatively flat organizational structures, there is no way to provide a career pathway. Luckily, there is. For example, career pathways can include milestones based on competency development and/or attainment of business goals that lead to a change in title. A Marketing Coordinator might become a Marketing Director. Recognition of career development is important. No one wants to feel stuck in the same role without recognition of what's been learned and accomplished. ⃗ **https://www.recruiter.com/i/4-ways-employers-can-build-big-career-pathways-in-small-companies/**.

Reflect Upon

Goal: Take time to focus on what you and your team need to keep growing

Reflect upon how your business is going to grow over the next 12-24 months and what critical skills (hard and soft) you will need to succeed?

Facilitate a "Best Part of My Job" internal campaign to allow your employees to reflect upon and share their own career stories. Ask them to reflect on how telling someone else the story impacts their perspective on the work and their

Recommended additional activities for companies with 51-499 employees

For larger companies, **consider how Managers can lead the "Best Part of My Job" campaign** (see above). If you have implemented "Career Champions" consider how they might help get this project started and ensure key themes are noted and brought into quarterly or annual business planning discussions when the topic of "people" or "team" is being discussed.

career. Share the results in a creative way that works for you, such as:

- A bulletin board with an image that represents each employee's story

- A newsletter that shares some of the stories

- A listing of what each employee's tweet would be if they had to sum up their career in 140 characters.

Measure

Goal: Identify good data that can help you make better business decisions

Other activities have asked you to identify metrics for training and career-related activities. **Bring all of the metrics across the activities together** and create a dashboard that ties the investment of time and funds to have employees participate in special projects aligned with key business goals.

Ensure to get employee feedback on how their work has enhanced their skills and competence in everyday responsibilities. You may want to start by gathering anecdotal evidence of how employees advance against career and business goals. After a few quarters, examine the pattern emerging and create a more quantitative dashboard to help you decide which employees and which projects deliver the best overall employee and company ROI.

The goal is to identify meaningful metrics that tie the career management activities you've identified with key business goals. After all, as Peter Drucker first said:

"There is nothing quite so useless as doing with great efficiency something that should not be done at all." ∎

Recommended additional activities for companies with 51-499 employees

This activity is best for companies that do employee engagement surveys. Often employee engagement surveys focus on how involved employees feel in certain company activities and how likely they would be to refer a friend or colleague to work at the company (part of what is called the net promoter score). **Employee engagement-related surveys can be enhanced** to help measure your company's career management maturity by adding the following to the end of any question being asked in the engagement survey: How important is this to you when considering your career goals?

When examining the responses you will see not only where employees are engaged with their work and your culture, but also where they feel an important item is being overlooked or undervalued by you. A lot of involvement in areas that don't tie to individual career goals may foreshadow engagement issues. Conversely, low engagement in areas that are very important to employee career plans can be linked to retention risk. In both cases, a career conversation that aligns company and employee goals is a good next step.

Template to Build a Small Enterprise Career Management Itinerary – Your Action Plan

My Career Management
Itinerary: (month) _____ , (year) _____ to (month) _____ , (year) _____

From Itinerary A: I will do **1** of the following anytime I have 10 minutes free in my schedule – list as many activities as you'd like to choose from:

	I Want to Do Next	I Am Doing	I'm Done	I Should Do Again
☐ _____	☐	☐	☐	☐
☐ _____	☐	☐	☐	☐
☐ _____	☐	☐	☐	☐
☐ _____	☐	☐	☐	☐

From Itinerary B: I will schedule a few hours per month to work on **2-3** of these activities each week for the next few months:

	I Want to Do Next	I Am Doing	I'm Done	I Should Do Again
☐ _____	☐	☐	☐	☐
☐ _____	☐	☐	☐	☐
☐ _____	☐	☐	☐	☐
☐ _____	☐	☐	☐	☐

From Itinerary C: Every few months, I will schedule a few hours in a block and work on **1** of these projects:

	I Want to Do Next	I Am Doing	I'm Done	I Should Do Again
☐ _____	☐	☐	☐	☐
☐ _____	☐	☐	☐	☐
☐ _____	☐	☐	☐	☐
☐ _____	☐	☐	☐	☐

Checklist:

Have you included activities from a variety of categories?

Think About	Share	Discuss	Do	Reflect Upon	Measure
☐	☐	☐	☐	☐	☐

If 1 activity leads to another, have you listed the follow-on activity as part of what you want to do next? _____

Do you feel confident to start all of the activities you have listed in the "To Do" or "I Am Doing" columns? If not, what questions do you have or what resources do you need?

_____
_____
_____

Who can help you answer your questions or find good resources? (**HINT:** Page 50 of this Playbook has a long list of resources for you in addition to your own colleagues, industry associations, Chamber of Commerce and company resources)

_____
_____
_____

Template to Build a Medium Enterprise Career Management Itinerary – Your Action Plan

My Career Management Itinerary: (month) _____ , (year) _____ to (month) _____ , (year) _____

From Itinerary A: I will do **1** of the following each day – select as many activities as you like:

	I Want to Do Next	I Am Doing	I'm Done	I Should Do Again
☐ _____	☐	☐	☐	☐
☐ _____	☐	☐	☐	☐
☐ _____	☐	☐	☐	☐

From Itinerary B: I will schedule **1** hour per week, when possible, to work on **2-3** of these activities:

	I Want to Do Next	I Am Doing	I'm Done	I Should Do Again
☐ _____	☐	☐	☐	☐
☐ _____	☐	☐	☐	☐
☐ _____	☐	☐	☐	☐

From Itinerary B or C: As part of quarterly business reviews, I will include **1** of these projects:

	I Want to Do Next	I Am Doing	I'm Done	I Should Do Again
☐ _____	☐	☐	☐	☐
☐ _____	☐	☐	☐	☐
☐ _____	☐	☐	☐	☐

From Itinerary C: As part of annual business planning, I will work on **1** of these projects:

	I Want to Do Next	I Am Doing	I'm Done	I Should Do Again
☐ _____	☐	☐	☐	☐
☐ _____	☐	☐	☐	☐
☐ _____	☐	☐	☐	☐

Checklist:

Have you included activities from a variety of categories?

Think About	Share	Discuss	Do	Reflect Upon	Measure
☐	☐	☐	☐	☐	☐

If 1 activity leads to another, have you listed the follow-on activity as part of what you want to do next? _____

Do you feel confident to start all of the activities you have listed in the "To Do" or "I Am Doing" columns? If not, what questions do you have or what resources do you need?

_____

Who can help you answer your questions or find good resources? (**HINT:** Page 50 of this Playbook has a long list of resources for you in addition to your own colleagues, industry associations, Chamber of Commerce and company resources)

_____

Sample Career Management Itinerary – Your Action Plan

My Career Management
Itinerary: (month) __July__, (year) __2018__ to (month) __January__, (year) __2019__

From Itinerary A: I will do **1** of the following anytime I have 10 minutes free in my schedule – list as many activities as you'd like to choose from:

	I Want to Do Next	I Am Doing	I'm Done	I Should Do Again
☐ _Call to check-in with a staff member_	☐	☑	☐	☐
☐ _Review staff training evaluations_	☑	☐	☐	☐
☐ _Search on LinkedIn or Glassdoor_	☐	☐	☐	☑
☐ _____	☐	☐	☐	☐

From Itinerary B: I will schedule a few hours per month to work on **2-3** of these activities each week for the next few months:

	I Want to Do Next	I Am Doing	I'm Done	I Should Do Again
☐ _Listen to "HR for Small Biz Podcasts"_	☐	☑	☐	☐
☐ _Set career-related business goals_	☑	☐	☐	☐
☐ _Consider having Career Champions_	☐	☑	☐	☐
☐ _____	☐	☐	☐	☐

From Itinerary C: Every few months, I will schedule a few hours in a block and work on **1** of these projects:

	I Want to Do Next	I Am Doing	I'm Done	I Should Do Again
☐ _Focus on better career conversations_	☐	☐	☐	☑
☐ _Create career pathways for sales team_	☐	☐	☑	☐
☐ _Learn more about triads and plan to intro to team_	☑	☐	☐	☐
☐ _____	☐	☐	☐	☐

Checklist:

Have you included activities from a variety of categories?

Think About	Share	Discuss	Do	Reflect Upon	Measure
✔	✔	✔	✔	✔	✔

If 1 activity leads to another, have you listed the follow-on activity as part of what you want to do next? __Yes__

Do you feel confident to start all of the activities you have listed in the "To Do" or "I Am Doing" columns? If not, what questions do you have or what resources do you need?

Not sure how to set career-related metrics that tie to business goals.

Who can help you answer your questions or find good resources? (**HINT:** Page 50 of this Playbook has a long list of resources for you in addition to your own colleagues, industry associations, Chamber of Commerce and company resources)

My accountant and bookkeeper
My Career Champions (research project for them)
Look for a training course on metrics
Ask Jill how her company does this

Section 4:
Special Situations

Special Situations

From time to time, situations arise that demand unique approaches. Here are tips and tools for you to use.

SME Owners told us that they felt employees need the most support career support during the early (39%) and mid-career (33%) stages while none of the Owners indicated that they felt employees in their late career stage or after significant absences needed specific support.

Several Business Owners declined to select a specific time when career issues emerge, instead, as an Owner said, "If you focus on the needs" of a group then you're doing a disservice to the employee. Each person needs attention when they need it not when you think they need it."

We agree and have recognized a few specific circumstances when employees may need additional attention and that present unique challenges for SMEs. You may want to go back to your template and add an action item from this section if these topics are relevant to your workforce. ∎

Losing Staff and Succession Planning

SMEs across the country told us that they struggle with balancing a sincere desire for staff to grow and to stay while retaining senior management or executive-level high-performers who are ready for the next challenge.

We hope that the activities and suggestions provided in the itinerary get some ideas flowing for how you can help your experienced staff continue to grow in their careers, even in a flat structure. However, even with an enhanced focus on internal career management activities, some of your staff will decide that they need to leave to meet career-related goals. Some will seek higher levels of responsibility, the opportunity to manage a larger team or budget or the chance to work in a new area or field. For others, geographic or family considerations may trigger the desire or need to move.

What happens if the right answer for a key employee is to leave? Is your business at risk?

In our interviews, 39% of Business Owners indicated that they never do any succession planning, while 50% indicated that it takes them between 3-6 months to hire a new Manager or experienced employee. If you knew that it would take 3-6 months to replace the revenue you earn from a key client, we doubt almost 40% of you would wait until the client ended their contract before starting new business development. ∎

VOICE OF A BUSINESS OWNER

"I got tired of people getting a designation (CA) and thinking they were going to do better outside because they didn't know there was room to grow here. So, I put in place a formal program (pathways to success) that is a tool to reduce unnecessary turnover. It facilitates conversations where employees can raise paths or next steps that are in the company that Managers don't realize they are interested in. The tools work. It is a way to retain good people."

TAKE ACTION:

On a quarterly basis, identify key employees who would be hard to replace should they decide to leave your company. Identify if it is their skills, relationships or other qualities that make them so valuable and consider who might be able to step into their role if they were ready to move on, either internally or externally. Make sure you keep these employees in mind as you review your Career Management Itinerary. Have you focused on engaging them in ways that will be meaningful?

TAKE ACTION:

SME Owners should ensure that they are maintaining their network and keeping strong relationships with Alumni (employees who have left the company) in order to maintain access to good, qualified referrals for new staff. You may find that employees who have left to pursue new career opportunities become great candidates a few years later for new roles, or they may be key customers and partners.

**VOICE OF A
BUSINESS OWNER**

"It is important for a SME to have no single point of failure. If 1 person is away, things cannot grind to a halt."

When Managers Are Not Comfortable or Capable of Having Career Conversations

TAKE ACTION:
In your Career Management Itinerary, there are suggested activities that assist with all 3 of these suggestions. Ensure you have thought of how you will support your Managers to have good, ongoing career conversations.

61% of Business Owners and Managers told us that they believe Managers find career conversations difficult.

In fact, only businesses with a high percentage of long-serving staff indicated that career conversations were easy for Managers. Perhaps this distinction is evidence that career conversations require a long-term focus within a trusted relationship. They are not transactional.

In our conversations, the top 3 reasons why career conversations are perceived to be difficult for Managers were due to:

- Limited financial resources to address specific employee compensation requests. "The conversation goes to compensation and we have little room to move."

- Limited knowledge of career-building experiences or emerging opportunities within their own organization. "Sometimes they don't even know where we're going so it's hard for them to explain to the employee where they are going in 2-5 years. In IT things are changing really quickly."

- Limited time to schedule a meeting, conduct the conversation and reflect on what the employee needs. "We are so busy working in the business and not on the business, so it's hard to find the time to find the space to explore and develop and I am just too busy trying to meet deadlines."

Business Owners did not seem concerned that their Managers lacked the skills to have sensitive, personal conversations with staff indicating confidence in the soft skills of their management teams. SME Managers need to wear many hats and develop strong internal and external relationships. They cannot rely on a large group of peers and Managers without strong people skills are unlikely to succeed.

Based on these findings, it seems evident that Business Owners can help enhance the quality of career conversations by:

- Providing non-financial recognition and reward suggestions to Managers in advance of meeting with employees.

- Considering how the business priorities and projects for the next 6-12 months might provide career-building opportunities for staff. Ensure Managers know which of these opportunities are available to staff.

- Helping Managers prioritize career conversations as a critical business activity. ∎

IMAGE: Qualities that Owners indicated make Managers better career coaches

DID YOU KNOW?

Good preparation for career conversations is critical, even when the staff member and Manager know each other well and have worked together for a long time. Here are 7 Pitfalls to avoid in career conversations (adapted from *Managing Human Resources: A Guide for Small Business Owners*):

1. Ignorance: Prepare for the conversation by reading the employee's file or reviewing their work. Look for unexplained gaps, contradictions or unfinished business. If this leaves you with questions, ask them and listen carefully to the answers.

2. Inattention: Do not allow interruptions during the conversation. Answering the phone or permitting disruptions insults your employee and undermines the value of the discussion.

3. Verbosity: Try not to talk too much during the discussion. Let the employee speak and listen carefully. Ask the employee what they want to talk about before dominating the agenda.

4. Inconsistency: Treat everyone the same. Stick to the same schedule or trigger point for career conversations. Maintain regular frequency.

5. Aimlessness: Covering irrelevant details reveals more about you than the employee. Try sticking with specific experiences and on-the-job examples to support your discussion.

6. Mismanagement: Always stay on track in the conversation. Stick to the time you had allotted, recognizing that you are committing to regular conversations. There should not be urgency to the discussion – this is a long-term ongoing relationship and discussion.

7. Procrastination: Don't take too long to make a decision. Keep your discussion process reasonable and non-bureaucratic. If you agree to do something set short-term and long-term time commitments for follow up.

Dealing with Life Events and Leaves of Absence

As we move into an era where there is increasing focus on work-life balance, there is a recognition that life events trigger unique career-related needs.

Sometimes an employee has asked for a leave of absence to care for a family member, or is taking maternity or parental leave. Other times, there has been a death in their family or other circumstances that lead to an interruption of their work. For SMEs, being flexible and addressing the career needs of your employees when they are off and after they've returned to work can be a challenge.

In Canada, 35% of the workforce is involved with caregiving for a family member. [21] The Federal Government has put together this list of practices that companies of various sizes are using to help address the needs of their employees, while addressing concerns related to productivity, staffing and turnover: **http://www.edsc.gc.ca/ fra/aines/rapports/ pcsean.shtml**.

CERIC has also published guides for both employers and employees that specifically address the career-related considerations when employees take maternity or parental leave. Many of the suggestions and recommendations in these guides are applicable to employees taking leaves of absence for other reasons.

Learn more at: **http:// ceric.ca/maternity_ employer** and **http:// ceric.ca/maternity_ employee**. ∎

 DID YOU KNOW?

According to Flexjobs, 82% of employees say they would be more loyal to their employers if they had flexible work options. [22] It is important to evaluate your workforce and workflow to determine if flex options, such as varied start times, teleworking and job sharing, are viable.

TAKE ACTION:

Review the materials recommended and consider that it is likely 1/3 of your staff are maintaining their current work schedules while balancing caregiving responsibilities. Decide if you want to add any actions to your Career Management Itinerary to research what the implications are in your specific organization, what your employees need and if there are hidden opportunities to satisfy your employee's needs while growing your business.

Career Considerations in Small- and Medium-Sized Family Businesses

Family businesses have additional unique dynamics to consider when implementing career-related activities.

There are 3 key considerations *Harvard Business Review* identifies for Owners of family businesses: [23]

1. Avoid conveying to children that there is always a place in the business for them. While the intent behind the message is good, it can lead to having employees who see their jobs as "fall-back" careers instead of something they have worked towards and chosen to grow.

2. Families tend to grow faster than businesses. This means that there may not be sufficient business growth to support the careers of every family member.

3. 2nd Generation employees tend to take on roles in the same area/function as their parent. Non-family members who aspire to leadership tend to gain broad functional and business experience and exposure. If 2nd Generation employees remain focused only in 1 part of the business they may not have the executive-level competencies required to take over leadership roles, if that is desired.

For non-family members, there are also career considerations. Family businesses are typically full of passion, challenge and commitment. If the vision of the company is to remain family-owned and operated, senior roles, such as CEO, may not be available. Frequently, certain roles or levels within the organization may seem to be restricted to family-members only.

For additional information and family

TAKE ACTION:

Recognize that good career management practices will ensure a more professional and predictable way to help employees identify and grow into roles within the company. Whether employees are family or from the outside, there is a need for open career conversations, transparency about future opportunities and an ability for staff to deal with Managers who can help bridge the employee's needs and goals with the business's best interests.

business resources, visit the Family Enterprise XChange **http://www.family-enterprise-xchange.com.** ∎

DID YOU KNOW?

According to the Family Enterprise XChange, "Family business is one of the oldest forms of commercial enterprise in the world with an estimated 80% of all businesses worldwide being family owned and operated. Current research demonstrates that, on average, family businesses last longer and outperform their non-family-run competitors and contribute upwards of 70-90% of global GDP."

Career Considerations for New Graduates

New graduates entering your company may not even realize the skills they offer and, without this awareness, it is easy to overlook them for new opportunities or consider them "not yet ready" to take on specific tasks.

There are many resources available to help ensure that you establish good working relationships with your newest employees, without relying on stereotype or generational assumptions to colour your interactions before you learn more about each other's work ethic, values and capabilities. For general tools, articles and discussion groups focused on hiring new grads, see: ☑ **http://talentegg.ca/ incubator/**. ∎

TAKE ACTION:

For new graduates that you are interviewing or hiring, the Career Centre at Laval University has developed a new, bilingual tool. It provides step-by-step guidance to new students and new graduates as they build a career portfolio: ☑ **http://www.webfolionational.ca/**.

DID YOU KNOW?

Research from the University of North Carolina shows that "Millennials want the same things from their employers that Generation X and Baby Boomers do: challenging, meaningful work; opportunities for learning, development and advancement; support to successfully integrate work and personal life; fair treatment and competitive compensation. What's more, all 3 generations agree on the characteristics of an ideal leader: a person who leads by example, is accessible, acts as a coach and mentor, helps employees see how their roles contribute to the organization, and challenges others and holds them accountable." [24]

Career Considerations for the 50+ Workforce

DID YOU KNOW?

According to AARP, "replacing an experienced worker can cost 50% or more of the individual's annual salary in turnover-related costs." [25]

The retirement age was set in the 1930s when life expectancy was 62.

Today, with life expectancy reaching into the mid-80s it is only natural that we see more and more employees choosing to work past the traditional retirement age. What's more, we know that many employees are worried about finances and need to continue earning income longer than they expected. The result is that a new phase of people's careers is emerging. Instead of moving from mid-career to retirement, people now transition with purpose from work that they did in their 30s and 40s into new work arrangements or positions that better align their talents, what they care about, their lifestyle and other needs and the market.

Like new graduates, there are many stereotypes, age-based assumptions and ageist language that dominate how "older workers" are viewed. Ageism in hiring

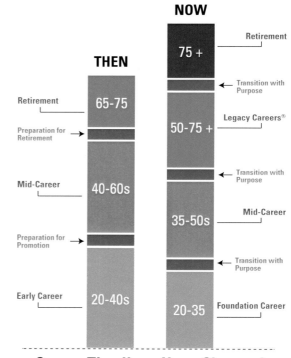

NOW

Retirement — 75 +

Transition with Purpose

Legacy Careers® — 50-75 +

Transition with Purpose

Mid-Career — 35-50s

Transition with Purpose

Foundation Career — 20-35

THEN

Retirement — 65-75

Preparation for Retirement →

Mid-Career — 40-60s

Preparation for Promotion →

Early Career — 20-40s

Career Timelines Have Changed
© Challenge Factory Inc 2012

practices is common, although, in most cases, it is unintentional. Simply put, we are not yet conditioned to consider our 60s and 70s as some of our most productive years. But, career timelines are changing and employers need to be aware that there are carrots (productivity gains, employee retention gains) and sticks (legal action, bad publicity) associated with outdated career thinking. ■

DID YOU KNOW?

According to a study conducted by the Center on Aging and Work at Boston College, "Results indicate that older workers (those 55 and older) are significantly more engaged than younger workers (those 54 and younger). In fact, employee engagement appears to increase with age among current cohorts who work in the retail environment we studied." [26]

TAKE ACTION:

Consider how your company is taking advantage of Legacy Career® talent. Ensure your older employees continue to have career conversations with your Managers – and ensure your Managers understand why these conversations are relevant and important. US-based "This Chair Rocks" and its blog "Yo, Is this Ageist?" provides free resources and current examples of how ageism affects everyone, everyday.
https://thischairrocks.com/. For workplace-specific questions, Challenge Factory is a North American leader in helping organizations capitalize on shifting demographics and provides many courses and resources for your staff and Managers at:
http://www.challengefactory.ca.

Section 5:
Listed and Additional
Resources

Career Management Resources for Business Owners

Many of the following resources have been referenced in this Playbook. They are organized here by topic for easy reference according to the various phases of your employee lifecycle.

Updated lists of resources as well as additional training and materials related to this Playbook can also be found at: http://www.challengefactory.ca/sme.

Hiring and Interviewing

A list of 31 competencies and related behaviours that can shape job descriptions, career conversations and development plans: http://www.workforce.com/2002/09/03/31-core-competencies-explained/

Wealth of articles focused on new graduates in the workplace: http://talentegg.ca/incubator/

Interactive tool designed by Laval University to assist new graduates in building career portfolios for hiring Managers: http://www.webfolionational.ca/

Variety of talent-related articles, tools and tips for entrepreneurs and start-ups: https://www.marsdd.com/tag/talent/

Articles focused on small business employee recruitment and management: https://www.bdc.ca/en/articles-tools/employees/pages/default.aspx

Building Your Culture

Variety of articles focused on small business employee engagement: https://www.marsdd.com/mars-library/motivating-employees/

Manager and Employee Guides to facilitate career conversations: http://www.crwg-gdrc.ca/crwg/index.php/resources/career-conversations

1,001 quotes that apply to small business and can generate great conversations within your company: https://www.amazon.ca/Quotes-Entrepreneurs-Great-Inspire-Motivate/dp/1496011252

Podcasts that cover a wide variety of HR-related topics – all from a small business perspective: https://itunes.apple.com/us/podcast/human-resources-for-small/id533673516?mt=2

Podcasts that focus on everyday employees sharing what they like about their jobs: http://www.bestpartofmyjob.com/podcast/

Communication

firm focused on internal/employee communication. Provides training for Managers and Owners to be better communicators: ☑ http://ow.ly/VBCz1oosfLk

Variety of talent-related articles, tools and tips for entrepreneurs and start-ups: ☑ https://www.marsdd.com/tag/talent/

Having Better Career Conversations

Article with 5 steps Managers can take to lead a career conversation: ☑ https://www.fastcompany.com/919177/dont-run-career-conversations

Virtual training platform with courses for employees, Managers and leaders. Especially relevant is Course 105, Better Career Conversations for People

Managers: ☑ http://ow.ly/hh2B1oouNXj

How to address limited upward mobility in small companies as part of broader career conversations: ☑ http://ow.ly/yn8I1ooy3Zv

Manager tools on how to have better coaching conversations: ☑ http://www.right.com/wps/wcm/connect/right-us-en/home/thoughtwire/categories/media-center/Two-Thirds-of-Managers-Need-Guidance-on-How-to-Coach-and-Develop-Careers

Checklist and tools for Managers to address performance management issues: ☑ http://hr.berkeley.edu/hr-network/central-guide-managing-hr/managing-hr/managing-successfully/performance-management/concepts

Articles focused on small business employee recruitment and management: ☑ https://www.bdc.ca/en/articles-tools/employees/pages/default.aspx

Retaining Talent

Articles focused on small business and start-up employee retention: ☑ https://www.marsdd.com/mars-library/retaining-top-talent-employee-retention-strategies-for-startups/

Checklist and tools for Managers to address performance management issues: ☑ http://hr.berkeley.edu/hr-network/central-guide-managing-hr/managing-hr/managing-successfully/performance-management/concepts

Article presenting data on the cost of turnover among senior staff: ☑ http://www.aarp.org/work/employers/info-06-2013/costs-of-employee-turnover.html

Variety of talent-related articles, tools and tips for entrepreneurs and start-ups: ☑ **https://www. marsdd.com/tag/talent/**

Training and Development

MARS Library with resources for Owners and Managers, including this sample evaluation form to measure the impact of training programs: ☑ **https://www.marsdd. com/mars-library/ training-evaluation- sample-feedback- questionnaire-for- trainees/**

Laval University: ☑ **http://www.ulaval.ca**

The G. Raymond Chang School of Continuing Education, Ryerson University ☑ **http:// www.ryerson.ca/ce**

Developing Leaders

Free, online assessment focused on career motivators: ☑ **http:// testyourself.psychtests.**

com/testid/3153

Best-selling book that supports leaders through having career conversations and engaging with employees: ☑ **https:// www.amazon.ca/ Help-Them-Grow- Watch-Conversations/ dp/1609946324**

A list of 31 competencies and related behaviours that can shape job descriptions, career conversations and development plans: ☑ **http://www.workforce. com/2002/09/03/31- core-competencies- explained/**

Communication firm focused on internal/employee communication. Provides training for Managers and Owners to be better communicators: ☑ **http://ow.ly/ VBCz10osfLk**

Variety of talent-related articles, tools and tips

for entrepreneurs and start-ups:

☑ **https://www. marsdd.com/tag/talent/**

Public relations and media training for Owners and Managers: ☑ **http://www. kekadasgupta.com**

Promoting from Within

Free, online assessment focused on career motivators: ☑ **http:// testyourself.psychtests. com/testid/3153**

Best-selling book that supports leaders through having career conversations and engaging with employees: ☑ **https:// www.amazon.ca/ Help-Them-Grow- Watch-Conversations/ dp/1609946324**

How to address limited upward mobility in small companies as part of broader career conversations: ☑ **https:// www.recruiter.com/i/4- ways-**

employers-can-build-big-career-pathways-in-small-companies/

Family Business

National organization with mandate to empower enterprising families and their advisors: ☑ **http://family-enterprise-xchange.com/**

Family advisory and succession planning firm: ☑ **http://edmondsrose.ca/**

Inter-Generational Workplaces

Research and consulting organization focused on the future of work and intergenerational topics: ☑ **http://www.challengefactory.ca**

Job board and resource centre for new graduates: ☑ **http://talentegg.ca/**

Anti-ageism activism and

resources: ☑ **https://thischairrocks.com**

Article debunking generational stereotypes: ☑ **http://about.beyond.com/infographics/Bucking-The-Stereotype-Millennials**

Article focused on intergenerational management issues and tips: ☑ **https://hbr.org/2013/05/hitting-the-intergenerational**

Inventory of employer-led flexible workplace practices that support employed caregivers:

☑ **http://www.esdc.gc.ca/eng/seniors/reports/cec.shtml#h2.10**

A study on the social values of Canadian millennials with a focus on work/career experience and aspirations:

☑ **http://www.environicsinstitute.org/**

Small Business Career Development Research and Findings

CERIC-supported collated content focused on career development: ☑ **http://www.contactpoint.ca/careerwise**

CERIC published text on topics related to career development: *Career Development Practice in Canada: Perspectives, Principles, and Professionalism*: ☑ **http://www.ceric.ca/textbook**

Canadian SME research report and recommendations: ☑ **https://www.bdc.ca/en/Documents/analysis_research/challenges-winning-strategies.pdf**

Section 6:
Thank You to
Our Knowledge
Champions

Knowledge Champions

A special thank you to our Knowledge Champions for career development who helped to make possible the publication of this Playbook.

 THE CANADIAN CHAMBER OF COMMERCE LA CHAMBRE DE COMMERCE DU CANADA

Canadian Chamber of Commerce

Since 1925, the Canadian Chamber of Commerce has connected businesses of all sizes, from all sectors and from all regions of the country. With a network of over 450 chambers of commerce and boards of trade, representing 200,000 businesses of all sizes we are Canada's largest business association; we foster business competitiveness and a strong economic environment that benefits all Canadians.
📄 http://www.chamber.ca

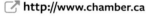  ceric
CANADIAN EDUCATION AND RESEARCH INSTITUTE FOR COUNSELLING
INSTITUT CANADIEN D'ÉDUCATION ET DE RECHERCHE EN ORIENTATION

Canadian Education and Research Institute for Counselling (CERIC)

CERIC — the Canadian Education and Research Institute for Counselling is a charitable organization that advances education and research in career counselling and career development, in order to increase the economic and social well-being of Canadians. It funds projects, hosts the Cannexus conference, publishes *The Canadian Journal of Career Development*, and runs the ContactPoint / OrientAction online communities.
📄 http://www.ceric.ca

 UNIVERSITÉ LAVAL

Laval University

Laval University, through its Career Centre (Service de placement) and Continuing Education, is proud to participate in the achievement of this publication intended for SME owners and managers. Thanks to its renowned expertise, our institution offers a continuum of services that concretely contribute to skills development and to the growth of Canadian businesses.
📄 http://www.ulaval.ca

 Ryerson University The Chang School of Continuing Education

The G. Raymond Chang School of Continuing Education, Ryerson University

Gain entrepreneurial skills and learn to grow ventures in a diverse marketplace with Ryerson University's G. Raymond Chang School of Continuing Education. With over 1,500 courses and 80 certificate programs to choose from, The Chang School is a leader in practical, applied learning that can advance your career today. 📄 http://www.ryerson.ca/ce

TD Community Giving

TD invests in communities to make a positive impact where it does business and where our customers, clients and employees live and work. In 2015, TD donated over $92.5 million to support community organizations in Canada, the United States and the United Kingdom. In Canada, we focus on Education and Financial Literacy, Creating Opportunities for Young People, and the Environment.

For more information, visit ⬀ **http://www.td.com/corporateresponsibility**

The CFO Centre

The CFO Centre is the leading global provider of part-time Chief Financial Officers for small- and medium-sized businesses. This concept allows smaller organizations to benefit from the expertise of a highly experienced Chief Financial Officer without incurring the expense of hiring someone full-time. There are no full-time fixed costs, no ongoing liability, just proactive advice, perceptive insight and hands-on support as and when needed. ⬀
http://www.thecfocentre.ca

CERIC is proudly supported by The Counselling Foundation of Canada.

The Counselling
Foundation of Canada

Notes and References

1. Statistics Canada, Business Register, December 2015.

2. Innovation, Science and Economic Development Canada, Key Small Business Statistics 2016. https://www.ic.gc.ca/eic/site/o61.nsf/eng/03022.html

3. 2016 Human Capital Benchmarking Report. Society for Human Resource Management, November 2016.

4. SMEs and Growth: Challenges and Winning Strategies, October 2015, https://www.bdc.ca/en/Documents/analysis_research/challenges-winning-strategies.pdf

5. 2015 Employee Engagement Benchmark Study, Tempkin Group, http://www.e-junkie.com/TemkinGroup/product/503553.php

6. Saba Fall Employee Engagement Study, 2015. https://www.saba.com/media/1040294/saba_employee-engagement_survey.pdf

7. The Great Divide Workforce Study, Beyond.com. http://about.beyond.com/infographics/Bucking-The-Stereotype-Millennials

8. Right Management. Manpower Group. http://www.right.com/wps/wcm/connect/right-us-en/home/thoughtwire/categories/media-center/Two-Thirds-of-Managers-Need-Guidance-on-How-to-Coach-and-Develop-Careers

9. Glossary of Career Development, ContactPoint, CERIC. http://contactpoint.ca/wiki/glossary-career-development/

10. All "Voice of an Employer" quotes are either from primary interviews that were conducted by Challenge Factory Inc. in 2016 or from Canadian Chamber of Commerce consultations in 2013. http://www.chamber.ca/media/news-releases/130220-canadian-chamber-offers-roadmap-to-close-small-business-skills-gap/

11. Markman, Art. "Why Career Development and Advancement Aren't the Same Thing," Fast Company, November 25, 2014. https://www.fastcompany.com/3038968/why-career-development-and-advancement-arent-the-same-thing

12. "Managing employee risk requires a culture of compliance," Gallup Business Journal, March 2016. http://www.gallup.com/businessjournal/190352/managing-employee-risk-requires-culture-compliance.aspx

13. Cornerstone Employee Engagement Survey (American data) https://www.cornerstoneondemand.com/news/press-releases/research-reveals-driving-force-behind-american-employees-and-their-career

14. "One in Three Employees claim to have a job rather than a career," Mercer 2015. http://www.mercer.com/newsroom/one-in-three-employees-claim-to-have-a-job-rather-than-a-career-new-mercer-survey-finds.html

15. SMEs and Growth: Challenges and Winning Strategies, October 2015, ↗ https://www.bdc.ca/en/Documents/analysis_research/challenges-winning-strategies.pdf

16. Berkley Human Resources, Concepts and Definitions. ↗ http://hr.berkeley.edu/hr-network/central-guide-managing-hr/managing-hr/managing-successfully/performance-management/concepts

17. Chapter 16: Lifelong Career Management in Career Development Practice in Canada: Perspectives, Principles, and Professionalism, January 2, 2014. CERIC. ↗ http://ceric.ca/resource/career-development-practice-in-canada-perspectives-principles-and-professionalism/

18. Career Development in SMEs: Needs Analysis, Canadian Research Working Group on Evidence-Based Practice Report 2, p, 62.

19. Adkins, Amy. "Only 35% of U.S. Managers Are Engaged in Their Jobs," Gallup Business Journal, April 2, 2015. ↗ http://www.gallup.com/businessjournal/182228/managers-engaged-jobs.aspx

20. Cornerstone Career Trends Report. Kelton Global. September 2015. ↗ https://www.cornerstoneondemand.com/sites/default/files/whitepaper/csod-wp-career-trends-report.pdf

21. Government of Canada. "When Work and Caregiving Collide: How Employers Can Support Their Employees who are Caregivers," Report from the Employer Panel for Caregivers, 2015.

↗ http://www.esdc.gc.ca/eng/seniors/reports/cec.shtml

22. FlexJobs 4th Annual Super Survey, August 2015, ↗ https://www.flexjobs.com/blog/post/survey-76-avoid-the-office-important-tasks/

23. Stalk, George and Foley, Henry. "Avoid the Traps that Can Destroy Family Business," Harvard Business Review, January-February 2012. ↗ https://hbr.org/2012/01/avoid-the-traps-that-can-destroy-family-businesses

24. Valcour, Monique. "Hitting the Intergenerational Sweet Spot," Harvard Business Review, May 27, 2013. ↗ https://hbr.org/2013/05/hitting-the-intergenerational

25. "What are the Costs of Employee Turnover?" American Association of Retired Persons (AARP), ↗ http://www.aarp.org/work/employers/info-06-2013/costs-of-employee-turnover.html

26. James, Jacquelyn B., Ph.D., Swanberg, Jennifer E., Ph.D., and McKechnie, Sharon P., Ph.D. Responsive Workplaces for Older Workers: Job Quality, Engagement and Workplace Flexibility. ↗ http://www.bc.edu/content/dam/files/research_sites/agingandwork/pdf/publications/IB11_ResponsiveWorkplace.pdf